Fruit Wedge Moon

Fruit Wedge Moon
Haiku, Senryu, Tanka, Kyoka, and Zappai

poems Richard Stevenson

photos Ellen McArthur

First Edition

Hidden Brook Press
www.HiddenBrookPress.com
writers@HiddenBrookPress.com

Copyright Layout © 2015 Hidden Brook Press
Copyright Text © 2015 Richard Stevenson
Copyright Photographs © 2015 Ellen McArthur

All rights for poems revert to the author. All rights for photographs revert to the photographer. All rights for book, layout and design remain with Hidden Brook Press. No part of this book may be reproduced except by a reviewer who may quote brief passages in a review. The use of any part of this publication reproduced, transmitted in any form or by any means, electronic, mechanical, photocopied, recorded or otherwise stored in a retrieval system without prior written consent of the publisher is an infringement of the copyright law.

Fruit Wedge Moon: Haiku, Senryu, Tanka, Kyoka, and Zappai
by Richard Stevenson

Cover Photograph — Ellen McArthur
B/W Photographs — Ellen McArthur
Cover Design — Richard M. Grove
Layout and Design — Richard M. Grove

Typeset in Calligraph 421 BT
Printed and bound in USA

Library and Archives Canada Cataloguing in Publication

Stevenson, Richard, 1952-, author
     Fruit wedge moon : Haiku, senryu, tanka, kyoka, and zappai / by Richard Stevenson.

ISBN 978-1-927725-29-0 (pbk.)

     1. Haiku, Canadian (English). 2. Waka, Canadian (English). I. McArthur, Ellen, 1946-, photographer II. Title.

PS8587.T479F78 2015   C811'.54   C2015-906830-4

for the Gorillas in the Mist/
(hot tub buddies supreme)/
and the Happy Hour/Remax/
dragonboat team/
"Paddles up!"

Preface

Fruit Wedge Moon. Remnant in an empty cocktail glass? Could be, except we're toasting the old girl with beer tonight. Five aging boomers, Gorillas in the Mist, rub a dub dubbing to our own dub beat in a hot tub. Right now Chief Silver Back is raising his beer stick above the 105 degree bubbles. It's forty below and his hair is frozen in a spiky punk fringe around a growing cul de sac... .

Could be a celebrated Japanese moon: harvest moon, chrysanthemum moon, fruit wedge moon... . Why not? These *haiku, senryu, tanka, kyoka,* and *zappai* — English language *haikai* poems and sequences, domestic, largely urban, play with the resources of the imagist, emblematic/shape, found, Kerouacian *pop* English language tradition, while paying homage to the original Japanese forms.

Specifically, the haiku, as currently practiced by most world *haijin*, is an imagist poem of up to, or slightly more than, seventeen syllables. Its traditional focus is nature or man in nature. It consists of a fragment and phrase juxtaposition of two images, delivered over three lines, which, like the two ends of a spark plug, create a spark of recognition, an ah-ha moment or epiphany, where the author's original experience is transferred directly, without the mitigation of figurative expression or ornament of any kind in simple present tense across the synapse of fragment and phrase. The diction is colloquial, plain. The form requires a seasonal word or reference (a *kigo*), a syntactic break, often accompanied by a dash, a comma, a colon, ellipses, or just white space in lieu of the traditional cutting word or particle (the *kireji*), usually after the first line, but often after the second.

Except that Japanese *on* or *onji* are not the same thing as syllables, and are of more even, clipped sound duration than are English syllables, which come in short, long, and Texan, hence making the one-breath-to-say-it rule sometimes difficult. Except that the 5-7-5 syllable distribution pattern is often padded with superfluous adjectives, adverbs, articles, or prepositions. Except that even the Japanese masters (Basho, Buson, Issa, Shiki, etc.) often broke most of the rules. Except that the Japanese wrote in one vertical rather than horizontal swatch in an ideographic rather than orthographic language ... etc. Except that the *avant garde* has moved its goal posts in one, two, three, four or more lines, and has managed, in one brilliant instance (Cor van den Heuvel's iconic 'ku, p. 18 (though appropriately unpaginated) in *Haiku in English: The First Hundred Years* edited by Jim Kacian, Philip Rowland, Allan Burns, with introduction by Billy Collins, Norton, 2013) to produce a single-word haiku, "tundra," which anticipates the language school abandonment of realism all together. Except, except, except... .

So nowadays seventeen syllables in English is considered by many English language haijin to be too long! Concision, one-breath poetry is the goal... .

The *senryu* had the same form but dealt with human nature in quick quips that consisted of ironic or sardonic observations, often in an urban landscape. A type of *senryu*, considered considerably more low brow by traditionalists, is the *zappai* which dealt openly, humorously, with frank, sexual subject matter or crude observations, or with subject matter considered inappropriate at high court society gatherings. I have found that it lends itself well to the found poem or English language graffiti *apercu*. Thus, a piece of bathroom graffiti — "My mother made me a lesbian. If I buy her the wool, will she make me one too?" or garage sign quip — " I used to go skinny dipping, but now I go chunky dunking" — are easily carved up and presented as *senryu* or *kyoka,* if one wishes to see how far one can stray from straight imagism and still compose a western minimalist poem.

Of course, a lot of folks have gone too far in abandoning any semblance to the haikai tradition, and create reams of puerile, veg-o-matic prose sliced and diced as pure abstract statements or Sunday school painterly description in three lines of 5-7-5 (so-called spamku, after the Internet proliferation of bad 'ku). That doesn't mean that folks can't raid the larder for the verbal equivalent of junk sculpture or write traditional Yiddish expressions or folk sayings in bad mother-in-law kvetching haiku strophes. So we get computer message and road rage and hockey spam-ku, some of which is at least amusing, and at best quite clever and witty. Not haiku or even senryu or zappai perhaps, but as found text or building blocks for a more traditional syllabic linked sequence, maybe not so much worthless or shop worn as one might presume.

Consider how the sonnet has evolved over the years. We now have fourteen-word sonnets or sound nets (Paul Dutton's so'nets), truncated sonnets, 15-line sonnets... .

The haiku as Basho introduced it was a truncated opening verse or hokku that served as the opening gambit of interactive chain-link associative 5-7-5 syllable, 7-7 rejoinder parlour games for two or more hands called *tanrenga, hakai no renga* or simply *renga* (from aristocratic parlour game roots) — later, renku (as practiced by regular citizens). Basho decapitated the verse and presented it as a micro poem. Along came Gary Gay in the twentieth century, who added a few of his own rules and restricted the number of passes and we now have the Rengay, a short *renku*.

Adaption, experimentation, play — not necessarily a Zen moment in which the compression of image and juxtaposed fragment and phrase resonate deeply, symbolically in a kind of *koan*, or function metaphorically and literally by process of allusion to other poems or tradition. Sometimes a high coo or snigger is all the doctor ordered.

The *tanka*, with its blessed two extra seven-syllable lines, was traditionally a highly personal and emotional lyric, and *tanka* were often written in cycles to a beloved, rather like sonnet sequences. It was an older form, rather like a truncated *hokku* & response link of *renku*, and wasn't so studiously avoidant of figurative expression or symbolism as a trope. As with the haiku, its five-line traditional structure divided in 5-7-5-7-7 syllables has become shorter and tighter in English, with its short (say, two beat) lines and longer (three beat) lines not necessarily being restricted to their traditional positions. Likewise, the subject matter has expanded beyond the erotic or romantic frisson to encompass a variety of tones and subjects.

The *kyoka* is to the *tanka* what the *senryu* is to the haiku: a more ribald, older, more profane human circus vehicle, often funny, deeply ironic, or sardonic, also originally written in a 5-7-5-7-7 syllable pattern of five lines. Great for social satire. It also mutated into shorter, more concise forms of alternating long and short lines in any order.

The sequences, patterned after traditional *renku*, are associative rather than narrative and proceed by accretion, though I've dropped any of the formalities or restrictions a host may require of his fellow *haijin* in calling image, tone, mood, or traditional links in the chain-link poem for two or more hands. Sometimes I've let slide the odd narrative, contextual link; usually, the title indicates the occasion or setting.

Fruit Wedge Moon, like its predecessor, *The Emerald Hour* (Ekstasis Editions, 2008) is a collaborative work set in southern Alberta — in my backyard, at neighbouring Henderson Lake Park and the Nikko Yuko Japanese Gardens, or at various locales in southern Alberta and BC (lower mainland and southern Vancouver Island mostly). As with the former work, Ellen McArthur and I decided to start with the text and break it up at regular intervals with Ellen's lovely black and white photographs. As with traditional haiga (sumi-e ink painting accompanied by a single haiku) or modern photo haiga, the intention isn't that the haiku caption any particular haiku, senryu, tanka, kyoka, or zappai or imply a directive narrative relationship, though, clearly, most of the haiku are set in the same southern Alberta locales where the pictures were taken.

Think of the photos as eye-ku. If you spend a little time with the images, you'll see many of the same framing devices, close observations, and interesting techniques — comparison, contrast, association, mystery (yugen), narrowing of focus, sketch, and focussing of the senses; the swing from macro to micro scale of the poems, or vice versa. In her praxis, Ellen ordinarily refuses to photoshop the image; rather, like the haiku, her image is composed in the process of seeing, framing the shot from a particular — often unusual — angle, at a particular time, and given specific lighting conditions. She modestly likes to say to me, "Who couldn't get a good shot at this beautiful location?" whenever we sit down to do a photo lay down. I don't see it that way: what I notice is the same questing intelligence that connects up the particular to something universal.

It's as if the rocks, the water, the trees, the clouds were speaking their own truths about nature and man's proper place in it. So rather than caption a particular photo with a specific poem, we tried to change up by modulating the tone and mood through a sequence of images in the way renku couple might make associative leaps from link to link in a sequence. We also wanted to open the door to random associations that are made by keeping image and word open to random retrieval, so anyone can start anywhere in the book and read a series of haiku or be with individual images and poems until the mind forms its own Gestalts. Anyone making a documentary film will tell you the same thing: don't announce the size and composition of the nails as they pass over the eye on a conveyor belt.

Somehow Ellen even manages to make pollution beautiful or see metaphor or symbolism in the particular patterns of growth or chance juxtapositions, and her sense of composition is superb. She has a similar sense of wit and whimsy to mine as well and is a pure delight to work with.

I've tried to follow Ellen's lead in responding to another art form — jazz — with poems that don't merely describe the sweep and majesty, or fragile lyric beauty, or anger and deep anguish of the themes, melodies, rhythms, counter rhythms, improvised solos of Miles Davis's and John Coltrane's ('Trane's) music in the jazz 'ku sequences; and I've tried to keep my eye on the full sensory panoply of images and events at the two festivals and link human nature to environment in leaping narrative in those particular music sequences as well.

Hopefully, the reader will find worlds in the small, the particular, the closely observed minutiae of our particular biome, and the photos and poems will begin to speak to each other in unexpected ways.

— *Richard Stevenson*

Table of Contents

Preface ... *p. ix*

– Boulevard Beluga ... *p. 3*
– My Cupcake Car ... *p. 20*
– Salmon Arm Roots and Blues Festival 2009 ... *p. 34*
– Cross Drift Moiré ... *p. 46*
– South Country Fair Suite ... *p. 88*
– Autumn Days: Jazz Pops For Jack ... *p. 97*
– Coltrane Pops ... *p. 102*
– Mugshots Club Sequence ... *p. 110*
– The Green Fuse Went Pfft ... *p. 111*

Acknowledgements ... *p. 115*
Previous Books & CD ... *p. 116*
Previous Chapbooks ... *p. 117*
Bio Notes ... *p. 118*

silent secateurs —
a cabbage white flutters
over the fence

(in memorium, P.K. Page)

*

'sissus? the boy asks —
such full-throated flowers
must surely reply

*

Battery Point —
gaggle garrison's
got it now

*

shovelling the walks —
a great horned owl waits to see
what I'll uncover

*

September breeze —
no rattle to the leaves
just yet

*

bare tree —
a piñata size owl
hoots my name

chinook —
the boulevard beluga
has a calf!

*

news of your death —
a second snowfall buries
my driveway

(for Gary Rumsby, 1952-2010)

*

the day lilies blare
red and orange arias —
still, no butterflies

harvest moon —
wife has hot flashes,
moons me!

*

cat box needs cleaning —
love that feminine ending
as she snicks the door

*

snow on
the upturned red wheelbarrow
d
e
p
e
n
d
i
n
g

*

Methlehem:
vacant, burned out homes, lots
of room in the inns

(after reading Nick Reding's
***Methland: The Death and Life of an American Small Town** (2009))*

*

wizened apples —
all the words I didn't say
still on the tree

*

granite erratic —
now a frosted muffin
in his front yard

(for Brian Bartlett)

cat box blues —
so much depends on
plastic's tensile strength

*

wobbly wasps stumble
from a rotten windfall —
sailors on shore leave

*

french fry sparrows —
too fat to fly south
of McDonald's lot

new coolness —
forest fire smoke makes the sun
the only ripe grape

*

forest fire smoke —
even the dragonflies
are grounded today

*

bumblebee stumbles,
wipes his six feet at the porch
of a hollyhock

second hand bookstore —
I find one of my recent books —
signed!

*

the hollyhock's got
bullhorn blossoms to croon
the bees to their knees
and a stadium reach
over monk's head and lambs ears

*

monk's hood ablaze!
shy milkmaid plants curtsey
behind the fence

I used to go
skinny dipping, but now I
go chunky dunking

(found senryu)

*

thirty below —
gorillas in the mist?!
no, hot tubbing men

*

flu flap —
funeral home lawn sports
an Open House sign

Value Village —
Va- LOO ViL-AJ for the
discerning shopper

*

"as is" gingko
back again for another
as is summer

*

the emerald hour —
each branch a boy with
a string of green fish

wearing mom's medal,
the little boy dragon boats his box
across Lake Lino

*

flu shot queue —
the lady in front of me
is missing three teeth
why do I think of bowling
at a time like this?

*

Sunday morning —
the choice of drifting snow
or banked mounds
of equally mum
student papers

tan, 'stache, and Stetson —
zen cowboy until the end —
the law took your meds;
you rode a dark mare
into the sunset

(for Bruce Henning, 1959-2010)

*

sunlit deck
the dachshund finds a spot
between leaves

*

twenty-seven years —
this sandwich she brings me
fresh as the first

(for Gepke)

suicide panache —
helium tied to his ears
razors in the sash

(with a wink to Robbie Newton Drummond)

*

something's died, you say,
and, sure enough, our daughter's
wrapped a dead bird
in a tissue shroud, stowed it
in a Singer drawer crypt

*

retriever, ginger cat
almost nose to nose
on age and hot stones

Playground Zone Ends —
a mountain ash holds its torch
of berries aloft

*

my old friend's dead —
I gaze at winter apples
clinging to the tree

(for Gary Rumsby, 1952- 2010)

*

three days of rain —
even the geese
leave their eggs

guitar neck inlay —
not mother of pearl
but mother of toilet seat

(Thanks, Daryll)

*

Boxing Day —
even the crunch of snow
sounds like Styrofoam

*

cumulo stratus —
an old woman cards wool
from her sheep

poet in rez
extolling my tricks
next to the Triskets

*

flu shot line —
Marilyn Monroe gets hers
up the tattoo wazoo

*

Christmas eve —
a charm of finches
form a single lung

classes over!
waiting in its staff lot slot
my cupcake car

*

tiny flakes falling —
as if the creator
were sifting flour

*

Halloween —
only thirty kids this year
happy to get pop,
then the older ones arrive
with black bags over their heads

flu shot line —
you'd think the kid ahead
were about to sit
on Santa's knee;
it's been that long a wait

*

cupcake roof —
shadows of branches
one hand grabbing

*

a murmuration
of starlings
doesn't murmur!

these needy runes
blasphemous as
footprints in the snow

*

magenta sun —
from forest fire haze
a province away

*

o
tramp   line —
now you see them;
now you don't:
heads' juggled pineapples
popping above the fence

power goes —
senryu's done

*

raging floodwaters —
a snake, a tree, a dead cow
float by the bridge

*

Maple Creek highway
now
a
wa
ter
fall!

sun ray on the sage —
a cabbage white opens
the petal of itself

*

our dachshund won't eat
sixteen hundred clams later
the vet presents
a shoelace, bits of plastic,
a swatch of towel

*

waking the dragon,
one boy moves eyes, jaws;
the other leaves food —
a horse-in-blanket routine
but — oh! —the black slippers

(Lethbridge Dragon Boat Festival)

we ring nine times
on the ninth hole
to rouse her ghost —
murder victim, the story goes
we want our own Betty Noir

*

cloud sheep lowing —
day lilies' lewd burlesque act
fails to attract
bon vivantes or butterflies,
so now they're on their bar stools.

*

three crows
in a young choke cherry tree
flap a lot to stay still

the emerald hour —
plump green tomatoes glow with
what the lilies shout

*

fence a fretboard
afternoon shadows slide,
leaves finger plink

*

still fountain —
a cottonwood seed
drifts overhead

(for Bruce Henning, 1959 -2010)

tee off —
lots of loft and distance
wrong fairway

*

fruit drink
with cherry blossom picture
a canned haiga

*

last day of classes —
day care kids on trikes
circle the pine

*

broken toe —
slow retreat of snow
along the boulevard

*

computer purr —
cat coils into sleep
in the desk chair

*

eaves dripping —
children's shopping cart
boasts a load of snow

canine porn?
knackered golden retriever
humps mini dachshund

*

begonia beguine!
such a scarlet floor show
descending these drab stairs

*

fork to glass clatter —
the wedding MC draws names
to see who will kiss

Salmon Arm Roots & Blues Festival 2009: A Haiku/Tanka Sequence

(for Marika)

weekend passes —
still, we boomers linger
over breakfast, lunch,
arrive in the late afternoon
ready to bop, ready to groove

*

fairground entrance:
an eagle aerie atop
a telephone pole

*

dancing dervish —
so entranced, in the moment
so alone

*

why no space
to dance in front of the stage?
every performer
has to ask the audience
are we having fun yet?

*

rodeo grounds —
barefoot dancers churn
horse shit and piss

*

tie dye shirts —
our son picks the one with
Rolling Stones logo

*

Johnny Winter!
chooses to sit while he plays
Boney Moroney

*

Trombone Shorty's
bullfrog cheeks expand, contract
on a three-note trill

*

Dr. John —
still the Creole shaman
points to each player
points two fingers at us
when he shuffles from the stage

*

Sam Roberts so loud!
better, clearer as we walk
back to the car

*

a toddler aims
his milk bottle at the sky —
trumpeter supreme!

*

grey-haired boomer
in floral pantaloons, still
the elfin dancer

*

thin, reedy voice —
sounds like *meow meow*
Tender Vittles ad?

*

soul man in a suit —
processed hair, Stax/Volt moves
fronts an X Gen band
shows all the performers
a thing or two

*

Bedouin Soundclash —
lead singer yells
to beer garden patrons,
*Break down the barriers!
Come out of your cage!*

*

Horace X —
black light thrum and weave
ska, reggae big beat;
a little two-tone, Slavic punk —
and dig the haberdashery!

*

The Soul of John Black
more than he can top, screw on
in porkpie Stetson

*

Souljah Fyah's
pop reggae one drop riddem
percolates like an old
Coleman stove-top coffee pot
while kids bop to a new groove

*

Youssuopha Sidibe's
one-too-many syllable handle
handily handled

*

Sidibe's kora
thumb piano-like notes
stroked, coaxed
from two sides of the neck,
two sides of the Atlantic

*

fusion groove —
Kries' lead singer
howls a Serb dirge;
puts a funk back beat
to a language we can eat

*

roots & blues —
first raffle ticket draw
a next year pass

*

main stage blocks away —
we watch the lead singer croon
on projection screens

*

gumboot gumbo —
our daughter not daunted
dances in gumboots

*

Iko Iko…
Dr. John's Crescent City
groove elation
has us all bouncin'
buns flexin' lawn chairs

*

hippie alley —
homemade soap moves slowly
in gumboot gumbo

*

glass beads and trinkets —
decent jembes, guitars,
all manner of
flotsam and jetsam,
Capistrano T's

*

caravan cuisine —
bills stick out of my wallet
like frog's feet

*

Rumba Calzada —
Habana/ Latino by
way of second gen
Filipino jazz, salsa,
Vancouver timbales, horns

*

roots & blues —
we choose our own
New Orleans gumbo,
season it with salsa,
drop riddem tzatziki

*

clouds keep us cool —
water water everywhere,
not a drop of rain!

*

Burroughs was right:
the Shits and the Johnsons
occupy two worlds
both point their lawn chairs
at the main stage

*

under a tarp
a young girl rolls a joint
a young mother frowns

*

same young mother dumb
enough to expose her toddler
to high decibels
never mind he's now confused
by brass milk bottle blues

*

what drug is this
that puts grannies in a trance?
hell, let's dance!

*

sun's out!
Admiral on a daisy cone
beats off a fly

*

Spooner's flutterby —
drifts by a mushroom bud,
passed by dragonfly

*

last adventure
before our daughter boards the
Kelowna-Comox
(via Edmonton) plane to
a new life away

*

tears at the airport —
our fledgling daughter newly schooled
ready to scoot

*

do you want
your fave trashy magazine
my wife asks
in our last half hour
before her flight

*

barn swallow swoops —
lumps in our throats as we see
our daughter aloft

* * *

family gone —
two cats sleep on the back
of the Chesterfield

*

weeks since your stroke —
the cubit coils of your hose
still hang in shadow

(in memoriam, Des Magrath)

*

a copse of alder —
so many soldiers
to commemorate

Dewey, Cheatam, and Howe —
should be a law firm,
but, no, it's a bar

(Thanks, Ellen)

*

blue sky!
paw prints at the windows
both sides of the glass

*

fruit wedge moon —
from the hot tub, the sky's
one full drink!

cornflower petals —
my old girlfriend's pom poms
punch the sky

*

gentle breeze —
the razzle dazzle rattle
of cottonwood leaves

*

jowls to sidewalk —
retriever's fine supine,
keeps an eye half-mast

Engleman's Ivy —
syllables as closely packed
as the leaves

*

dragon boat practice —
gulls above the park trees
cruise for burgers

*

no one home at last,
but the neighbour's weed whacker
whacks these words flat

finch Twitter:
so many Tweets
I'm not privy to

*

last to leaf out,
the ash's lime green leaves shout
popsicle bouquets

*

family gone —
retriever's nose prints along
the front window

glucose meter —
hard to believe happiness
can have a number

*

snoring dachshund —
my own breath rises
and falls to his tune

*

tittering finches —
a man with a black backpack
walks past my window

Bell Express VU —
as good a perch as any
robin decides

*

Cessna overhead —
the robin cocks its ear
to new vibrations

*

edge of the ice —
a plastic baseball bat
among willow snags

black clouds moil —
still, robin chortles atop the
tall
est
cot
ton
wood

*

dachshund barks —
thence the big street blockin' beats
of daughter's jeep

*

geese calling,
or some cop or car alarm?
too overcast to tell

dragon boat races —
dachshund twists and turns in
his own dragon dance

*

pine martin tracks —
each bounding series
a *karumi* Braille

*

catch, pull —
the gentle plash of paddles
in time today

(*dragon boat practice, Henderson Lake, Lethbridge*)

trees still in bud —
an ant pauses before
a cigarette butt

*

cool zephyr —
the time even litter
has some place to go

*

red cupcake
on the boulevard —
my son's first car

dandelions up
before grounds crews decide
they're not flowers

*

not twa corbies
but two magpies atop your elm's
dendritic reach

*

wife gone, kids asleep —
first cup of coffee
fogs my glasses

house viewing —
magpies play pick-up-stix
with lawn-strewn twigs

*

first chainsaw roar —
robin's cutting chortle trill
blows our guy off stage

*

two healthy elms —
no plaques or tangles
in senior's parking

restless night —
sudden smell of rosemary
in the cat's fur

*

backhoe berm —
ant pauses before pieces of
broken pottery

*

wasp huzzah —
dachshund turns his butt
the other way

Cross-Canada Trail:
sign at the head link
says no parking please

*

blue sky —
jet contrail's stay-puffed *l*
fades to mist

*

plus thirteen —
Canada Geese wait
for the ice to melt

first rabbit of spring —
that pause when neither of us
makes a move

*

nippy this morning —
the dog stops to read each
and every tree

*

first summer rain —
the lilacs flounce a little
over the fence

unseasonable snow —
robins pick at last year's
wizened apples

*

satellite dish —
six icicles drip
from six channels

*

book launch —
some dirty snow still
hugs the curb

Sunday in the park —
kids and caboodle,
even a poodle!

*

from one tree
aspen's winter thought
in dendrite and root

*

the usual
confectionery of snow —
and one magpie!

fatal stroke—
boulevard-parked cars
form a bouquet

(for Des Magrath)

*

plumbing truck sign:
"a flush trumps
a full house"

*

titter of finches —
weeping birch glow against
filigree snow

my students don't smile —
   irony deficiency
      this time

   (Thanks, Keith)

                *

   such honking —
you'd think the lake were
   a stock room floor!

                *

   handicapped girl —
   Dodi Wan Kenobi
   in her zipped parka

   (Thanks, Quenton)

Battery Point —
Canada geese flotilla
sends two point men

*

tatters of snow —
children screech and spin
on the park tire swing

*

corn snow —
not quite hail
not packing peanuts

cross drift moiré—
Bible camp kids
swarm the sundeck

(Crowsnest Lake, AB)

*

first growl of thunder —
dachshund sniffs the gravel
for his own scent

*

half moon —
dog's bark above
the factory noise

breaking up talk —
boyfriend's car parked
facing the street

*

sick in bed —
birds' silhouettes make whole notes
on the power lines

*

church atop the hill —
hawk glides in smaller circles
above the swather

I'm going outside —
to see what's on the nature
channel, he said

*

clank of iron —
two butterflies ascend
in their mating dance

*

dead head —
that's the secret,
she said

(Thanks, Ellen)

empty white chair
at the edge of the meadow —
a tape measure click

*

rattlesnake cairn —
our own park inukshuk
of erratic stones

*

death mask?
a crumpled plastic bag
in the bare branches

plastered with bird shit—
the old school piano
still gives us a C

*

son on drugs?
more mud than sand
in the sand bar

*

little windfall apples —
cartoon cherry bombs
that went pffft

grey after rain —
still the lilacs shout
we're whiter than white!

*

lady's mantle —
rhinestone raindrops
on every leaf!

*

semester over!
a butterfly lands on
the skill saw blade

among new buds
last year's bird nest
a kind of chalice

*

pink snow —
already the cars fashion
new ruts in the road

*

"Busy Gal,"
the license plate says —
she primps in rear view

tawny coulee —
against the wind, cicadas'
insistent whir

*

prickly pear —
hidden in golden grass,
still green and holding

*

chamomile —
even in the deepest ruts
your dry, sweet smell

off-leash dog run —
both dogs still grinning
all the way home

*

ah, grasshopper,
such a robust click of wings
for such tawny hills

*

dead end street —
iridescent grackle's
gold eye glints

Lighthouse Gospel Church —
crow atop a cross tops
a pre-fab trailer

*

ten o'clock —
you'd think the roosters would be
tired of their own noise

*

inland sea?
no, a field of flax
amid winter wheat

bracken fern,
thimbleberry, and beer can —
home at last!

(Victoria, BC)

*

the emerald hour —
shadows' one big glove waits
for a pop fly sun

*

weathered teak
and an old swag lamp globe —
my tea light moon!

* * *

South Country Fair Suite:
A Haiku / Senryu Sequence

(for Adrian)

kids in the river —
swallows follow the insect
thermocline up, down

*

before the festival
a young kid's river beer
drifts apart, away

*

meet lobster boy —
slept on his left side
in the sun, poor guy

*

fifty seven —
the river current seems
faster this year

*

rooftop patio —
my only guest the sparrow
that eyes my muffin

*

swallow acrobatics —
conductor's fevered baton
note for note no match

*

fast-moving water —
we joke about opening
a single shoe booth

*

stage set-up —
we follow the space station
passing the stars

*

messiah sans thorns —
the hippy's neon headband
changes colours

*

too many 'shrooms —
lobster boy's eyes his only
moving part today

*

laser lights, dry ice —
ladies and gentlemen,
Neanderthals live!

*

fortune teller's booth —
the love triangle triad
visibly shaken

(for Quenton, Deana, and Verna)

*

huge inner tube —
and in the middle, the girl
three boys woo

*

tattoos and tits —
might as well be cookies
on a country plate

*

bagpipe serenade —
what intrepid camper could
miss that reveille?

*

skull on a pole —
that's one way to find
your way home

*

Gina Drag Piper —
plaid scrotum, priapic pipes —
gives a jig a go

*

grass weed-whacked meek —
not so the luxuriant hair
on the lady's legs

*

Go ask Alice —
her umbrella hat makes her
the biggest mushroom

*

carnie atmosphere —
a hippy hides two beer
under his shirt

*

henna tattoos —
and just down the beaten path
new spoon jewellery

*

here they come:
bottles, plastic sandals,
tampon applicator?!

*

poetry stage —
a guy in a funny hat
pretends he's black

*

too hot to sleep in —
a boy's right face and arm
bake a ying/yang man!

*

making long distance
calls to Ralph and Beulah —
no great white phone

*

pierced Buddha bellies —
still scarfing candy apples,
sporting purple hair

*

a long tattoo sleeve
under the dress shirt —
his punk band phase

(for Lance)

*

radiant search lights —
a bug suddenly gets
a centre spot

*

"kitchen bitch" :
my latest moniker earned
for camp site omelettes

*

cognac and good dope —
we plot a sixties sitcom
pilot episode

*

breakfast burritos —
swallows carve at the sky
with rosined bows

* * *

Autumn Leaves: Jazz Pops for Jack

Zucchini chubber!
From across the alley
guitar runs and riffs

*

"So What?"
The languid hips in it —
that's it!

*

The emerald hour
Coltrane stretches the notes
on "Miles' Mode"

*

Coals to Newcastle
a paper wasp with green plans
in a rolled leaf

*

apples pink-cheeked
plump finches titter a bit,
peck out the bass

*

cymbal sizzle breeze
blue jay screeches wee-eee! wee-ee!
and down come the leaves

*

Heads up, Ornette!
Autumn leaves got nothin'
on blue boppin' jay!

*

softer than cymbals
splayed sprinkler streams
on zucchini leaves

*

Turn down the blaster!
Rap's got nothin' on
this sprinkler patter

*

quick pitter patter
around the kit, this sprinkler's
chick a chick so-oo hip!

* * *

a stiff breeze
red-cheeked apples
drop snicker snack

*

rock in the park
action dachshund's just gotta
do his solo too!

*

rock steady dachshund
you just can't compete
with electric blues

Coltrane Pops

Coltrane's "Greensleeves"
the old cat curls up
next to my laptop

*

Coltrane's soprano
searching among chords
cat's ears swivel too

*

The classic quartet's
"It's Easy To Remember"
old cat's eyes close

*

'Trane's "Out of This World"
keeps the cat's ears piqued
and peepers open

*

Tyner comps under
the silver splash of cymbals,
Coltrane's alley sax
searching paper bags and cans
out in these mean bass streets

*

Tyner's finch fingers
titter in the cymbal splash
of falling waters
while 'Trane's tenor weeps
of home from a farther shore

*

'Trane's acetylene torch
slowly seals seams of "Miles' Mode"
this gun metal day

*

'Trane! You're so sly
even the discordant notes don't
make the cat's ears flinch

*

Tyner cavorts now
cat's ears trained
on the laptop fence

*

Rim shot! Cymbal splash!
Cat's ear pivots toward
the sun-splashed shores.
Who's rowing this awful boat
toward the Godhead now?

*

Tyner comps
under scintillating cymbal splash,
bass's heron reach

*

Coltrane mellow on
"Nancy (With The Laughing Face)"
cat stretches a paw

*

What's new? Honey?
Cat's pure marmalade
in his jar of dreams.
Coltrane's tenor torch probes
for holes between the notes

*

"Up Against The Wall"
the classic quartet acquits it —
self most seamlessly

*

Trane's tenor travels
down seamless silver track
cat just licks his paws.

*

"I Wish I Knew"
Tyner's keys keep crooning
under horn quest

*

Love, you call it
the first movement in which
Tyner tickles God

*

sometimes a cat yowls
not now, your sax searching
for alley scraps

*

a cat yowling,
some might say, but a light
came on, didn't it?

*

discordant, harsh
yet the acetylene blues
cut through steel

*

Rim shot! Splash!
You take the tiller on tenor,
stars' canopy
acceding passage
of your pea green boat

*

Joy, the third movement
your horn's mother calling you
from the back porch still

*

Cats in heat
caterwaul from God's alley
for moon's milk saucer

*

The big C
man, you hadda know;
you hadda blow!

*

Tenor terrorist!
You come out blazing bullets,
spray the audience

*

raw as a dog's nose
chasing down rabbits
tenor hound howling

*

blackboard finger notes
got the bare moon bone
clamped in your jaws

*

sugar is sweet
taproot tenor sucks and shucks
huckleberry wine

*

sheets of sound
so many rain/sleet notes
so many windows

*

Big C
Chasin' the Trane
finches in the eaves

*

Look out, Jericho!
Got an ax that'll blow
leaves off the trees;
gotta a blow torch
and acetylene will!

* * *

Mugshots Club Sequence

finger splint —
guitar player can still
play slide!

*

*Hey Babe,
take those home to Hazel!*
thong hangs from the mic

*

panties on stage —
*I see your underwear,
raise you a jock strap*

*

poetry's a gift —
that's why you can't sell it,
a friend avers

* * *

the green fuse went *pfft*
you would think the dachshund nabbed
a live cherry bomb

*

last stage lung cancer —
my friend tells me how much
more deeply he reads

(for Gary Rumsby, 1952 — 2010)

*

ten years
since the family broke bread
Dad on another planet

grackle on a snag —
dachshund more interested in
my cheese and cracker

*

green thought green shade
cottonwood sputnik seed
on yard recon

*

three baby robins —
even Edward G never
looked so toady

* * *

Acknowledgements

Some of these poems previously appeared in/on the following journals, (electronic) magazines, anthologies, e-books, CDs, and chapbooks:

American Tanka, Atlas Poetica, Autumn Leaves, Berry Blue Haiku, Blue Skies, Chrysanthemum, DailyHaiku.org, Elan, a Regina Weese Collection (Wingate Press, ON, 2005) A Gaggle of Geese (chapbook), **Haiku J, Haiku Page (Yazoo River Press), Haiku Pix, Haiku Reality, Haiku Sun, Happano no Koba** (Ongoing **Fragments** Anthology), **A Hundred Gourds, Jazz Pops for Jack** (chapbook from **Laurel Reed Books**, 2010), **Kohinoor, Lynx: A Journal for Linking Poets, Lyrical Passion E-zine, Mu Haiku Journal, Neon Headband** (chapbook from **Leaf Press**, 2012), **The New Pleiades Anthology of Poetry** edited by Richard Vallance (Describe Adonis Press, 2005), **Notes from the Gean, Prune Juice, Rags, Riverbend Haiku, Seven by Twenty, South by Southwest, tinywords, Vancouver Cherry Blossom Festival web site** (Honourable mention),**Whirligig, Writing the Land: Alberta Through Its Poets** edited by Dymphny Dronyk and Angela Kublik (House of Blue Skies, 2007), and **Zen Haiku Canada.**

My thanks to the editors for their encouragement and support.

Previous Books & CD:

Driving Offensively (Sono Nis Press, 1985)
Suiting Up (Third Eye Publications, 1986)
Horizontal Hotel: A Nigerian Odyssey (TSAR Publications, 1989)
Whatever It Is Plants Dream ... (Goose Lane Editions, 1990)
Learning To Breathe (Cacanadadada Press, 1992)
From The Mouths of Angels (Ekstasis Editions, 1993)
Flying Coffins (Ekstasis Editions, 1994)
Why Were All The Werewolves Men? (Thistledown Press, 1994)
Wiser Pills (HMS Electronic Books, 1994)
A Murder of Crows: New & Selected Poems (Black Moss Press, 1998)
Nothing Definite Yeti (Ekstasis Editions, 1999)
C4/4 Miles* (a Muse 'n' Blues Production of Sound Gallery Enterprises, 1999) with poetry/jazz troupe **Naked Ear** and composer Gordon Leigh
Live Evil: A Homage To Miles Davis (Thistledown Press, 2000)
Hot Flashes: Maiduguri Haiku, Senryu, and Tanka (Ekstasis Editions, 2001)
Take Me To Your Leader! (Bayeux Arts Inc., 2003)
A Charm of Finches (Ekstasis Editions, 2004)
Parrot With Tourette's (Black Moss Press, Palm Poets Series, 2004)
Alex Anklebone & Andy the Dog (Bayeux Arts Inc., 2005)
Riding On a Magpie Riff (Black Moss Press, memoir for their **Settlements** series, 2006)
Bye Bye Blackbird: An Elegiac Sequence for Miles Davis (Ekstasis Editions, 2007)
The Emerald Hour: Haiku, Senryu, Tanka, and Zappai , with photographs by Ellen McArthur (Ekstasis Editions, 2008)
Tidings of Magpies: Haiku, Senryu, and Tanka (Spotted Cow Press, 2008)
Wiser Pills (Revised Edition, Frontenac Editions, 2008)
Windfall Apples (Athabasca University Press, 2010)
Casting Out Nines (Ekstasis Editions, 2011)
The Haunting of Amos Manor (Palimpsest Press/ Magpie Books, 2011)
A Dog Named Normal (Ekstasis Editions, 2013)

Previous Chapbooks:

Hierarchy At The Feeder (dollarpoem editions, 1984)
Twelve Houseplants (dollarpoem editions, 1985)
Dick and Jane Have Sex (greensleeve editions, 1990)
Fuzzy Dice (Cubicle Press, 2004)\
Frank's Aquarium (Cubicle Press, 2004)
Flicker At The Fascia (Serengeti Press, 2005)
Tempus Fugit (Laurel Reed Books, 2005)
Jazz Pops for Jack (Laurel Reed Books, 2011)
Neon Headband (Leaf Press, 2012)

Author Bio Note:

Richard Stevenson has just retired from 30 years of teaching English and Creative writing at **Lethbridge College** in southern Alberta. His other haikai collections include **Hot Flashes**, **Tidings of Magpies**, **A Charm of Finches**, **Flicker at the Fascia**, **The Emerald Hour**, **Windfall Apples**, and **Casting Out Nines**. His most recent other work includes a juvenile novel, **The Haunting of Amos Manor** (2012), a lyric/narrative free verse collection **A Dog Named Normal** (2013), and two chapbooks, **Neon Headband** (2012) and **A Gaggle of Geese** (forthcoming).

Photographer Bio Note:

Ellen McArthur has been a passionate photographer since her eldest was very small. As her youngest is now 44, well ... we'll let you do the math. Her other artistic endeavors include pen & ink, pencil, watercolour and creating the most astonishing cheesecakes. She & her husband live in Lethbridge, Alberta, along with the most incredible young man for whom they provide care. Rounding out this domestic scene are four box turtles. Ellen & Richard have been friends for many years & have collaborated on previous works, most notably, **The Emerald Hour** by Ekstasis Editions.

www.ingramcontent.com/pod-product-compliance
Lightning Source LLC
Chambersburg PA
CBHW081350080526
44588CB00016B/2445